Flowers for the Unborn Baby
A Biblical Look At Abortion
Gilbert James

Into Thine Hand
Publishing with a biblical perspective
4141 NW 39th Ave
Fort Lauderdale, FL 33309
www.intothinehand.com

Flowers for the Unborn Baby
A Biblical Look At Abortion

Published by
Into Thine Hand
4141 NW 39th Ave
Fort Lauderdale FL 33309
www.intothinehand.com

ISBN: 978-0-9841231-4-8

Flowers for the Unborn Baby

A Biblical Look At Abortion

Let's Celebrate the Upside

Let us focus on the upside Yes, the upside of a wonderfully designed human being who has been blessed with the gift of life. All of the attempts that may have been waged have been unsuccessful at winning over your life. You don't have to pinch yourself. The fact that you are able to read this booklet means life. Whether you consider it a blessing or otherwise, that has zero bearing on the fact that your domicile has not been transferred from the upside to being an oc - cupant of the downside or the grave.

Whether you gave the credit to your undaunting resilience or that of the involvement of divine guidance, you are here, on the upside You can earn millions going forward. You can change lives, especially yours. You still can choose and refuse to accept that which is detrimental to your life and your dreams.

Today serves as either the beginning or furthering of a living breathing chapter in your future condition of life or horizon. You have been given the gift of "from this point on" contributing to your life and your quality of life lived.

As we focus on the inside it is an undeniable fact that both genders of the human race, a male and a female coming together in one union have been able to produce a life That is how it has been re - volving ever since the beginning of the human race. That is how you and I came into being and the cycle goes on.

That life established the fact that you and I have been so wonderfully designed by the combined genes of the two life re-contributors, the two human beings, the male and the female, whose genes we are.

Though the greater burden appears to be placed on one side of the contributors the female who is given the grand opportunity of carrying that life for nine months, the contribution is actually of equal importance and responsibility. The real reason is because without the contribution of both entities, the production of life cannot and

6

could not be designed.

With the combination of the two, life is and is in the processing of developing in the womb into stages of unpredictable productivity. This includes the movements and learned traits from the womb to the entrance into the outside world and beyond.

The apprehension regarding the potential of the direction of the developing life is real and in reality, a developing mystery. Though the potential exists for the mystery to unfold into an undesirable direction, this mystery existed in all of our horizons from conception to destination.

The fact that we are here clinches the fact that we were given that opportunity to witness the revealing of or the unfolding of that mystery. That is the cycle of the human race. That is the cycle of life. That is the cycle of our existence.

Proliferation is the cycle of the human race. It is the cycle of life. It is the cycle of the revolving population of this earth.

As we venture into the biblical look at abortion I trust that you will lend yourself to the uncovering of the overwhelming reasons why just as you and I were given the opportunity at life the cycle should and must continue.

Table of Contents

Number of Abortions - Abortion Counters

Each real-time abortion counter is based on the most current statistics* for the number of abortions in the US & the number of abortions Worldwide.

US Abortion Clock.org

In United States today	**United States this Year**	**Worldwide since 1980**
1,594.0	163,588.4	1,447,064,991
US since 1973: Roe vs Wade	**US this Year after 16 weeks gestation**	**Worldwide this Year**
59,279,583.4	7,852.2	7,148,952
By Planned Parenthood since 1970		**WW since you loaded this page**
7,666,577.4	**US this Year due to rape or incest**	383
By Planned Parenthood this year	1,586.8	**Worldwide Today**
57,226.4		68,827
	Black babies since '73 in US	
	17,783,875.0	

3/4/2017 3:04 PM   http://www.numberofabortions.com/

"In October 2016, Planned Parenthood turned 100 years strong. Planned Parenthood was founded on the revolutionary idea that women should have the information and care they need to live strong, healthy lives and fulfill their dreams — no ceilings, no limits."
https://www.plannedparenthood.org/about-us/who-we-are

This quote was taken directly from the Planned Parenthood website 03/04/17 at 3:52pm

To grasp the true limitless nature of the real operation of the Planned Parenthood agenda, take a discerning look at the bold type above. Yes, they do mean that women should have the information and care they need to live strong, healthy lives and fulfill their dreams — no ceilings, no limits.

This includes the limit of the women's unwanted pregnancies which consists of removing the unborn baby out of the way up to what they call viability which is debatable between 23-28 weeks of the pregnancy.

Regardless of the other mentioned services of Planned Parenthood, abortion is among their top level services that they do on a wholesale level, yes as they noted, without ceilings, without limits for the woman.

You can usually identify them by their signature "Women's Centers" in your local neighborhood.

It is Just A Little Game... I Win, You Lose, That's It!

Fact: Abortion will not solve any relationship problems you now have nor will it hold together an unstable relationship. It is very common for relationships to break up shortly after an abortion.

Fact: Abortion doesn't make babies "go away." It kills them. If that bothers you, you'll feel much worse later.

Fact: Immediately after an abortion, a woman will usually feel re lieved. However, that is not the end of the story. What is over is the baby's life At some future point, the mother will become aware of this and then she may have to deal with grief and guilt.

Fact: Abortion is forever. You can't ever get your baby back.

Case Histories

- Mary, thirty years old and pregnant, had a chronic physical illness and strongly wanted an abortion. After the abortion she experienced guilt and self-hatred and called it "the least desirable solution".
- Joan was seventeen when she had her abortion. She seemed to cope well. But during her second pregnancy she "heard" babies crying at night and the pain came back to her.
- Sixteen year old Alisha had an abortion while high on drugs. A year later she came to feel that no one could love her because she had "killed her baby". Her solution was to get pregnant again, although she didn't know which boyfriend would be the father.

These cases are taken from psychiatrists' casebooks and crisis in tervention hotline logs. The names are fictitious: the problems are real, the source reported. Source – Life Cycle Books USA Fort Collins, CO 80522 https://www.lifecyclebooks.com/store/usa/downloadable/download/sam ple/sample_id/14/ Contact the listed source for any further details or assistance.

What Is The Definition of Abortion?

The real definition of abortion is found within the pages of the book of Jeremiah chapter twenty and verse seventeen. Here is what it says: "Because he slew me not from the womb; or that my mother might have been my grave, and her womb to be always great with me."

The prophet Jeremiah, in this scripture passage was throwing a pity party for himself as he, with self-sympathy, reasoned why God did not slay him in his mother's womb or make his mother's womb his grave.

However, the process that he described is the biblical reference to the modern day process of abortion. It is actually slaying the child from the mother's womb. It is the process where the mother's womb becomes the child's grave.

Of course, God did not do that because that's not what He does. To the contrary, He saved the prophet Jeremiah for His predestined use and purpose for his life as He wants to do for each unborn child. This includes yours, mines and all others.

Is Humanity A Divinely Endangered Species?

The scripture tells us in Geneses nine verses five through six the following: *And surely your blood of your lives will I require;* **at the hand of every beast** *will I require it, and* **at the hand of man; at the hand of every man's brother** *will* **I** *require the life of man. Whoso sheddeth man's blood, by man shall his blood be shed:* **for in the image of God made he man.**

Please note that God requires the life of the animals for the life of mankind. That rules out the theory of man being a type of animal. Though some behavior of the animal is typical to that of the human being that does not make it a type of human beings or human beings a type of it. The fact that the birds eat, drink, express the need for love and care does not make them a type of cat that has the same needs. That rules out the theory of man evolving from the animals which would have made the animals the primary ge netic base for humanity.

Even in most countries today, especially in the United States, when an animal bites a human or takes the life of a human, the authorities come in and takes the life of that animal... WHY?

The scripture states in Romans one verses nineteen through twenty the following: *Because that which may be known of God is manifest in thepfor God hath shewed it unto them.* For the invisible things of him from the creation of the world are clearly seen, being understood by the things that are madę *even his eternal power and Godhead; so that they are without excuse:"* Notice where that which may be known of Go is manifested: in them, that is in mankind. We know, because our Creator made us in His image and wrote His laws within our hearts.

Romans two, verses fifteen through sixteen admonishes us as follows: *For* **when the Gentiles, which have not the law, do by nature the things contained in the law,** *these, having not the law, are a law unto themselves:* **Which shew the work of the law written in their heartş** THEIR CONSCIENCE *also bearing witness, and their thoughts the mean while accusing or else excusing one another.*

Most importantly, God requires the life of the human beings for the life of man (mankind). This means that at the end of the abortion, God requires the life of all those who took part in the act for the life of that baby which is a human being. We will talk more about that later.

The answer given by the maker of mankind for requiring life for the life of the human being is because man was made in the image of God. Nothing is said here about man being the higher animal,

God sets man apart and distinct from the animals This takes us right into the realm of CAPITAL PUNISHMENT for taking the life of a human, including that unborn baby.

In case you were asking if the Bible supports CAPITAL PUNISHMENT the answer is YES, IT DOES! God gave the government the power to take revenge for evil on earth, not just anyone. Romans thirteen verses one through four says: *Let every soul **be subject unto the higher powers**. For there is no power but of God: **the powers that bare ordained of God.** Whosoever therefore resisteth the power, resisteth the ordinance of God: and **they that resist shall receive to themselves damnation** For **rulers are not a terror to good works, but to the evil.** Wilt thou then not be afraid of the power? do that which is good, and thou shalt have praise of the same: For **he is the minister of God to thee for good** But if thou do that which is evil, be afraid; for he beareth not the sword in vain: for **he is the minister of God, a revenger to execute wrath upon him that doeth evil.***

The Word of God embraces civil punishment but not vigilantism. As we saw, God gave the power to avenge the offense against the human life to the powers that be That is the government. The other entity, other than the government or the powers that be that is authorized by the scriptures to take vengeance upon those who offend humanity or the society is divine vengeance or punishment. This is substantiated by the writings of the apostle Paul in the book of Romans twelve and verse nineteen where he wrote: *Dearly beloved, avenge not yourselves, but rather give place unto wrath: for it is written, Vengeance is mine; I will repay, saith the Lord.*

How interested is God, the Creator, in the Unborn?

In the first place, He, that is God, is the one who forms the child in the womb In the book of Isaiah chapter forty four and verse twenty four we find these words: *Thus saith the Lord, thy redeemer, and he that formed thee from the womb, I am the Lord that maketh all things that stretcheth forth the heavens alone; that spreadeth abroad the earth by myself;*

God not only forms the child in the womb, He both calls from the womb and makes reference to the child, by name, in the womb before birth. Examine the following reference in the scripture. Isaiah forty nine verse one states: *Listen, O isles, unto me; and hearken, ye people, from far;* **The Lord hath called me from the womb from the bowels of my mother hath he made mention of my name** If God not only gives the child a name but addresses the child by his name in the womb, then He who is his creator considers the child to be a worthy person from the womb.

The Lord both knows of the child's existence in the womb and sanctifies or sets the child apart in the womb for His purpose. The book of Jeremiah chapter one and verse five brings that out. It says: **Before I formed thee in the belly I knew thee and before thou camest forth out of the womb I sanctified thee** and **I ordained thee a prophet unto the nations.** Notice that in God's economy, He knew the child before the womb. Notice also that God sanctified or set the child apart and ordained or placed His approval on him as a prophet or for an office in His work.

God is the designer of the structure of the human in the womb. This is what the scripture says in the book of Job thirty one and verse fifteen: *Did not* **he that made me in the womb make him** *? and did not one* **fashion us in the womb** Verses eight through ten of Job ten not only confirms but expands on the direct involvement of God, the Creator in the development of the child in the womb. It says: **Thine hands have made me and fashioned me** *together round about; yet thou dost destroy me. Remember, I beseech thee, that* **thou hast made me as the clay;** *and wilt thou bring me into dust again?* **Hast thou not poured me out as milk and curdled me like cheese** *Thou hast* **clothed me with skin and flesh, and hast fenced me with bones and sinews.**

These are not abstract but concrete terms: made and fashion. These speak to deliberate and direct designing by the Creator. Poured me out as milk curdled me like cheese clothed me with skin and flesh, fenced me with bones and sinews This speaks of the entire process of the germination, growth and development of the child in the womb to the point of the child being delivered from or exits the womb.

In the book of Genesis chapter one verse one, the Bible used the word create or the Hebrew word Bara' (baw-raw') which means to create something out of nothing. It says *"In the beginning God cre-ated the heaven and the earth."* The use of the word Bara' is relatively consistent throughout Genesis one in relation to God's creation. The same word was used in relation to Him creating mankind in Genesis one verse twenty seven which states *"So God createdman in his own image, in the image of Godcreated he him; male and female created he them."* The same word Bara' (baw-raw') was used in all three instances in the verse.

In Genesis two and verse seven, the Bible used the Hebrew word Yatsar (yaw-tsar') which means to form, fashion or frame. *"7. And the Lord God formed man of the dust of the ground, and breathed into his nostrils the breath of life; and man became a living soul."*

This is the same word used in Isa. 44:24 and Jer. 1:5 in relation to the unborn child. In Gen. 2:22, the Bible uses the word Banah (baw-naw') a slightly different word from the word Bara' (baw-raw') used in Geneses one in relation to the creation of the heavens and the earth and that of the male whom he created. The new term Banah (baw-naw') was used in relation to the woman whom God made from the rib taken out of man, which means to build, rebuild, establish or cause to continue *"22. And the rib, which the Lord God had taken from man, made He a woman, and brought her unto the man."*

The writer has not seen that word used again in relation to mankind in subsequent scripture passages. In Gen. 1:26, the Bible uses the word hX[`asah (aw-saw') which means to fashion, accomplish or make "*26. And God said, Let us **make** an in our image...*"

This is the same word used in Job. 31:15 and Job 10:8-9. In relation to the unborn child. Back in Gen. 1:27, the Bible uses the word Bara' (baw-raw') in relation to both the male and female, which means to create something out of nothing This could be because the female is still considered a part of the human race which He created with His own substance that was not existing before He create it.

Since the same words used in Geneses in relation to the process of creating mankind is used in reference to the process of the conception and development of the unborn child, IS GOD ACTIVELY CREATING TODAY IN LIGHT OF THE ASSERTION IN GENESIS THAT GOD FINISHED THE CREATION IN SIX DAYS AND DECLARED THAT ALL OF IT WAS GOOD? Or is the conception and development of the unborn child just a process resulting from the scientific laws that God has established?

To conclude that God is in the process of another creation subsequent to the Genesis account is far-fetched at best.

To conclude that the process of the conception and development of the unborn child is exclusively based on the scientific laws that God has setup is theistic evolution... which PROPOSED THAT GOD CREATED THE SCIENTIFIC LAWS OF EVOLUTION AND LEFT THE UNIVERSE TO OPERATE ON ITS OWN LAWS which is not supported by the scrip ture.

However, to assert that God is actively involved in process of the germination, including the process of the conception and development of the unborn child is in line with scripture.

This position is supported in the book of Colossians chapter one verses fifteen though seventeen which states: *15. Who is the image of the invisible God, the firstborn of every creature: 16. For by him **were all things created**, that are in heaven, and that are in earth, visible and invisible, whether they be thrones, or dominions, or principalities, or* *powers: all things were created by him, and for him: 17. And he is be fore all things, and **by him all things consist (held together).***

God owns the child in the womb and ordains the protection of the child in the womb. The book of Psalms one thirty nine and verses thirteen through sixteen speak to this fact. It states the following: *For thou **hast possessed my reins** thou hast **covered (to administer protection or covering or to weave together) me in my mother's womb**I will praise thee; for **I am fearfully and wonderfully made** marvelous are thy works and that my soul knoweth right well. **My substance was not hid from thee when I was made in secret, (hiding place, shelter, secret place, secrecy)**and curiously wrought in the lowest parts of the earth. **Thine eyes did see my substance, yet being unperfect (embryo Unformed); and in thy book all my mem bers were written**which in continuance were fashionedwhen as yet there was none of them.*

For a child of God or any human being to assert that God sanctions, or even allows abortion, the killing of the unborn child is doing a grave disservice to the Creator and His Word. It is to totally misconstrue the point intended by God.

When or at what point in the pregnancy does the unborbecome a child?

From Westchester Institute for Ethics & the Human Person: When Does Human Life Begin?

> Resolving the question of when human life begins is critical for advancing a reasoned public policy debate over abortion and human embryo research. This article considers the current scientific evidence in human embryology and addresses two central questions concerning the beginning of life: 1) in the course of sperm-egg interaction, when is a new cell formed that is distinct from either sperm or egg? and 2) is this new cell a new human organism—i.e., a new human being? Based on universally accepted

scientific criteria, a new cell, the human zygote, comes into existence at the moment of sperm-egg fusion, an event that occurs in less than a second. Upon formation, the zygote immediately initiates a complex sequence of events that establish the molecular conditions required for continued embryonic development. The behavior of the zygote is radically unlike that of either sperm or egg separately and is characteristic of a human organism. Thus, the scientific evidence supports the conclusion that a zygote is a human organism and that the life of a new human being commences at a scientifically well defined "moment of conception." This conclusion is objective, consistent with the factual evidence, and independent of any specific ethical, moral, political, or religious view of human life or of human embryos. http://www.westchesterinstitute.net/resources/white-papers/351-white-paper

From National Right to Life Foundation: When Does Life Begin? The life of a baby begins long before he or she is born. A new individual human being begins at fertilization, when the sperm and ovum meet to form a single cell. If the baby's life is not interrupted, he or she will someday become an adult man or woman. Worldwide, millions of unborn babies are killed each year. In the United States over 40 million unborn babies have been killed in the 29 years since abortion was legalized and more than 1.3 million are killed each year (equals to 37.7 million for the 29 year period). http://www.nrlc.org/abortion/wdlb/wdlb.html

Pro-Life America: Life Begins at the Beginning (A Doctor Gives the Scientific Facts on When Life Begins)
By Fritz Baumgartner, MD April 12, 2005

Dear Friend,

We can approach abortion from many perspectives: Biological, embryological, genetic, philosophical, social and economic, at the very least. As for the first three – my approach as a scientist, physician, surgeon, and simply someone who finished medical school, is factual.

There is no more pivotal moment in the subsequent growth and development of a human being than when 23 chromosomes of the father join with 23 chromosomes of the mother to form a unique, 46-chromosomed individual, with a gender, who had previously simply not existed. Period. No debate.

There is no more appropriate moment to begin calling a human "human" than the moment of fertilization. And don't let anyone tell you otherwise, because it would be a degradation of factual embryology to say it would be any other moment.
http://www.prolife.com/life_begins.html

What does the Bible say about the question of when or at what point does the child becomes a human being? In the book of Luke chapter one verse thirty six the Bible says "And, behold, thy cousin Elisabeth, she hath also conceived a son in her old age: and this is the sixth month with her, who was called barren." Notice that Elisabeth conceived a child. Notice also that the child's gender was determined and identified at conception: She conceived a son. No amplification of the stipulation is necessary. The words are direct and to the point: "she conceived a son." The child was a son at conception.

Are there any direct biblical commands against abortion?

The scripture says in Exodus twenty one verses twenty two through twenty four the following: *"If men strive, and **hurt a woman with child, so that her fruit depart from her**, and yet no **mischief** follow: **he shall be surely punished, according as the woman's husband will lay upon him**; and he shall pay as the judges determine. And **if any mischief follow, then thou shalt give life for life."**

The term mischief used here, refers to the death of the mother or the carrier of the child. I also believe that it refers to premeditated action on the part of the instigator, regardless of dual or single loss. Based upon the stipulations outlined here, at least civil litigation is perfectly in order for the loss or the death of the child in the womb. It is the writer's understanding that the limit to civil litigation is only if the infraction was accidental upon the woman or the mother of the child. Consequently, if the infraction on the mother of the child was premeditated, then mischief was present. It is my belief that mischief is also present when the action resulting in the loss of the child or the mother was premeditated.

In the case where the premeditated action on the part of the instigator(s) resulted in the loss of the child or the mother, mischief is present and criminal actions are the appropriate pursuits. In the case where there is no premeditation and the child alone dies, then civil litigation is the appropriate pursuit. However if the mother or the carrier of the child is lost in the process, whether premeditation is present or not, then criminal litigation is the appropriate pursuit.

The scripture is very clear in the book of Genesis chapter nine verses five through six regarding the requirement by the Creator of mankind for the taking of a human life. This includes the taking of the life of the unborn child which is also a human being. The passage said: *And **surely your blood of your lives will I require at the hand of every beast will I require it**, and **at the hand of Man, at the hand of every man's brother will I require the life of man.** Whoso **sheddeth man's blood, by man shall his blood be shed for in the image of God made he man (mankind).***

20

Since the child becomes a human being at the point of conception, consequently, the taking of that life whether in the womb or any time there after should constitute murder.

Should the administrators of the abortion get the death penalty as prescribed in the scriptures for murder?

As we briefly looked at earlier, the scripture stated clearly in the book of Geneses nine verses five through six that for taking the life of a human being, God requires life in return. This is because, as is clearly stated, man was made in the image of God as against any other creature.

So if we accept the unborn child to be a human being, who is, and God requires life for the taking of the life of a human being, it is clear that God requires life for the taking of the life of the unborn child

Let's examine further Amos 1:13 – *'Thus saith the Lord; For three transgressions of the children of Ammon, and for four, I will not turn away the punishment thereof; because they have ripped up the women with child of Gilead, that they might enlarge their border:"*

In this passage, we see that God has a passion for the sanctity of the life of the women carrying their children in the womb. He stated that for those who initiate harm to the woman carrying her child in the womb, He would not turn away their punishment. The specific harm at hand is murder. Of course, it is a given that murdering the mother would include the child.

Though the scripture puts a high bounty of life on the life of a human, because we are made in the image of God, the scripture in this passage appears to be sounding a very loud alarm on the murdering of a woman with a child in her womb. It is as if God placed an even higher premium on the murdering of a woman with child, which includes the child she is carrying.

Notice further, in the book of Exodus chapter twenty three verse seven. The scripture states the following: *"Keep thee far from a false matter; and **the innocent** and righteous **slay thou not** for I will not justify **the wicked.**"*

Here the cry is for the innocent and the prohibition is to slay them not or not to slay them. Would you consider the unborn child the innocent or the guilty? If the latter is your conclusion, what offense has the unborn child committed? The undisputed answer, I am sure you will agree is absolutely none.

Secondly, at the end of an abortion, is the unborn child slain or ends up dead (murdered)? Consider further, if God requires life for the slaying of the human being and the life of the unborn child, who is a human being, is taken, what would you consider the punishment to be? The answer should be clearly understood.

However, since God places the responsibility upon the powers that be to punish the offender and the only other entity who is authorized to take vengeance, as He said vengeance is mine, ultimately, we would have to leave it into the hand of one of those entities to avenge the life of the unborn child.

On the other hand, God used the prophets, the people and the re ligious authorities through biblical history to call out the unconscionable lifestyles of civil authorities. The big question for Christendom right now is where are we in our roles of calling out the unconscionable lifestyles of the civil authorities for the wholesale slaying of the innocent unborn child?

The scripture stated further in the book of Deuteronomy chapter twenty seven and verse twenty five the following: ***Cursed be he that taketh reward to slay an innocent person** And all the people shall say, Amen.*

If you were to start itemizing the people that make a living out of the slaying of the innocent unborn child, I wonder how close home with this take us? Would it take you out into the medical field, in your local community, your family, your home or even yourself?

Would you considered a person who places his/her career over the life of the unborn child among, those who are rewarded for the slaying of the life of the innocent unborn child? Did your choice of the career that was chosen over the life of the innocent unborn child gain you a greater salary (if so assumed) than if you had kept yourself "uninvolved" with the death of the unborn child? Would you consider that being rewarded for the slaying of the innocent unborn child? I trust that the result of your calculation would clearly point to the fact - truth of this matter. That is that indeed, choosing ones career over the death of the innocent unborn child is being rewarded for the slaying of the life of the innocent unborn child.

Since no aborted child has been proven guilty as yet, as such they are considered innocent until proven guilty. Consequently, are the administrators and facilitators of abortion guilty before God? If so, what are the authorities doing to protect them and set them free from the unproven punishment of death that thy experience daily?

Should a child conceived as a result of rape or incest be aborted?

Does the scripture have anything to say about that subject, directly or indirectly? Believe it or not, the scripture speaks "directly" to that subject. In the book of Deuteronomy twenty four and verse sixteen, the scripture says: *The fathers shall not be put to death for the children,* **neither shall the children be put to death for the fathers every man shall be put to death for his own sin**.

The truth of the matter is that this language is very straight forward. It provides no room for discussion or condition. The mandate falls into the realm of being very dogmatic.

So what if the parents made a bad judgment? No room was given for us to discuss the whys or the circumstances surrounding the pregnancy.

So what if the father or mother committed a sin, any sin, in the process of conceiving the child? The scripture unfortunately for many of us who would like a way out of seeing the unborn child come to full term and being born into this family, no exception was provided. In other words, no way out was provided. You and I can fill in the blanks regarding any exception, motive or circumstances. None will fit.

Should the child who may be born de formed or retarded be aborted?

Based upon the scriptural answer, God also made the deformed or retarded, if you please. Examine Exodus chapter four verse eleven which says: *And the Lord said unto him, Who hath made man's mouth? or **who maketh the dumb, or deaf** or the seeing, or **the blind? have not I the Lord?***

When I examined verse twelve of that same chapter, I find that God was able to use Moses who indeed had a lisp tongue to where it is believed that he stuttered in his speech. This was a speech impediment which resulted from a deformity that Moses had.

Look at the magnitude in which God was able to use Moses in the life of the Israelites. Moses was known as one of the big guns in the sight of the children of Israel and in the sight of God. What if he were aborted just because he was deformed in some way.

Is the dumb, the deaf, the blind a deliberate make of God, their Creator? God, the Creator of mankind does not do coincidence. If He made them, and He said that He did, it is a conscious deliberate shot.

The human being (the designed) is not given the luxury of being able to question the Creator (the designer) regarding the design that He delivers. Examine what the scripture says in Isaiah chapter forty five and verses nine through ten: **Woe unto him that striveth with his Maker!** Let the potsherd (earthenware, clay pottery, shard, earthen vessel) strive with the potsherds of the earth. **Shall the clay say to him that fashioneth it, What makest thou? or thy work, He hath no hands?** Woe unto him that saith unto his father, What begettest thou? or to the woman, What hast thou brought forth?

From this passage, it is clear that deformity is not a justified reason for abortion.

This truth is reinforced more in the book of Romans chapter nine and verse twenty. It says: Nay but, O man, who art thou that repliest against God? **Shall the thing formed say to him that formed it, Why hast thou made me thus?**

Here God is identified as the one who is not to be questioned. Why? Because He is the maker or the one who does the forming of that which is formed.

Does the parent have the right to control the child's fatal destiny?

The scripture speaks to the fact that the children ultimately belong to the Lord and parents are just stewards assigned by the Lord. Examine what the scripture says in Psalm one hundred and twenty seven verse three: Lo, **children are an heritage of the Lord** and **the fruit of the womb is HIS reward.**

Here, the power to determine the removal of the life of the children, born or unborn, is snatched from the hand of the assigned and rests in the hand of the assigner. The reason is that they are His heritage which makes Him the rightful owner of them all. They are His reward which established the fact that if the assigned takes away the life of one of them, he/she has removed God's reward instead of the as-Signed's

This undeniable right of the owner to determine the lethal fate of the life of the child, born or unborn, is reinforced by the writings of the prophet Ezekiel in chapter eighteen and verse four of his book. It says: *Behold, **all souls are mine; as the soul of the father, so also the soul of the son is mine** the soul that sinneth, it shall die.*

Here the scripture speaks in no uncertain terms. It leaves no room for man to claim ownership of the right to take the child's life. It specifically says that all souls belong to the Lord. It went on to specify that the soul of the father is the Lord's as the soul of the son (child).

Please examine further the words of the psalmist in Psalm one hundred and thirty nine and verse thirteen which says: *For **thou hast possessed my reins** thou hast covered me in my mother's womb*.

Let us notice first of all that the possessor of the reins of mankind, both in and out of the womb is God Almighty, the Creator. Notice further that as the owner, he covers or protects the child in the mother's womb instead of destroying them. So there is absolutely no grounds for the assigned to assume the Creator's role nor do to the unborn child what the Creator wouldn't do to His own which is to kill them in the womb. Instead, He protects them, He covers them.

Where does the aborted or any dead child go – heaven or hell?

What did David say about the destiny of his child after death that sheds light on where the unborn babies are in eternity? Let's examine second Samuel twelve verses eighteen through twenty three. The passage states the following: *And it came to pass on the seventh day, that **the child died** And the servants of David feared to tell him that the child was dead: for they said, Behold, while the child was yet alive, we spake unto him, and he would not hearken unto our voice: how will he then vex himself, if we tell him that the child is* *dead? 19. But **when David saw that his servants whispered, David perceived that the child was dead: therefore David said unto his servants, Is the child dead? And they said, He is dead.** 20. Then David arose from the earth, and washed, and anointed himself, and changed his apparel, and came into the house of the Lord, and worshipped: then he came to his own house; and when he required, they set bread before him, and he did eat. 21. Then said his servants unto him, What thing is this that thou hast done? **thou didst fast and weep for the child, while it was alive; but when the child was dead, thou didst rise and eat bread.** 22. And **he said, While the child was yet alive, I fasted and wept: for I said, Who can tell whether God will be gracious to me, that the child may live?** 23. But **now he is dead, wherefore should I fast? can I bring him back again? I shall go to him,** but he shall not return to me.*

When the child was sick, David fasted and wept over the child's condition but when the child was dead, he got up, had the table set and ate bread. However, notice what he said regarding the eternal state of the child in verse twenty three: **now he is dead, wherefore should I fast? can I bring him back again? I shall go to him**, but he shall not return to me The key statement is '**I SHALL GO TO HIM,**" but he shall not return to me.

David affirmed that the child was with God, which is where he would go when He died. He had hope of seeing the child again after death, though the child wasn't going to come back to him while he was alive.

Let us also examine Jesus' take on where children go when they die. In the book of Matthew chapter nineteen and verse fourteen, Jesus made the following statement: *But Jesus said, Suffer little children, and forbid them not, to come unto me: **for of such is the kingdom of heaven.***

Notice that Jesus loved and welcomed children, more specifically, as He specified, '**little children.**" It is the writer's understanding from the words of Jesus that He was referring to children who have not reached the state of accountability to where they can responsibly accept Christ as their Savior.

This also goes from the oldest state of non-accountability back to conception. Notice that I did not use the term "age of accountabil-lty" because different children mature at different age. The age of accountability for some children may be different for others.

It is clear that Jesus was saying in the passage under discussion that little children will go to be with the Lord when they die because **"of such is the kingdom of heaven."**

Is abortion the solution to an unplanned pregnancy?

The book of Isaiah made reference to a factor in the nature of the makeup of the female that rules out abortion being a solution to her unplanned pregnancy. Let us examine what is said in Isaiah chapter forty nine and verse fifteen: *Can a woman forget her sucking child, that she should not have compassion on the son of her womb? yea, they may forget,* **yet will I not forget thee.**

Though the speaker, who was God, affirmed the remote possibility that a woman may forget her suckling child, the tone of the passage was that this is an exception and not her true nature. It is the writer's understanding from the passage that the key message resonating from it is that a woman does not ever forget her suckling child as a norm but rather the exception.

As such, the act of abortion could come back to haunt the woman throughout the rest of her life. The reality is that there are more po-tential experiences and symbols that will show up throughout the rest of a woman's life which will serve as reminders of her missing child than not.

Deep counseling is usually required to truly orient the abortive mother into functioning status again. The most appropriate of the means that will serve to orient the abortive mother into somewhat functional lifestyle is to confess the sin and repent severely.

A pastor of a Bible believing church, a Christian counselor, a mature Christian woman are appropriate entities to consult for assistance in recovering and moving on before the Lord. A spiritually gratifying end result is possible with careful efforts of restoration.

What will never serve as a solution is not confessing it and continue to keep it a secret. This strategy is to continue to live with the guilt which could continue to haunt the abortive mother for a long time, possibly for a lifetime.

Is there any room for a life after an abortion, in the church?

The answer is emphatically yes! God is the God of second chances and third and fourth and seventy times seven. Jesus said in Matthew eleven and verse twenty eight *"Come unto me, all ye that labour and are heavy laden, and I will give you rest. Take my yoke upon you, and learn of me; for I am meek and lowly in heart: and ye shull find rest unto your souls. For my yoke is easy, and my burden is light."*

You can place the burden of abortion upon Jesus Christ. He will take it from you and give you rest from it all. His yoke is easy, He said and His burden is light. You can find true rest if you give it all to Jesus.

This same Jesus stated further in the book of John chapter six and verse thirty seven *"All that the Father giveth me shall come to me; and him that cometh to me I will in no wise cast out."*

He stated clearly in this passage that the one who comes to Him, He will not run you away. To the contrary, He will take them in. He will welcome us with all our sins, including abortion.

Let's remember that God used a few murderers mightily throughout the scriptures. Remember that Moses was a murderer. He killed the

Egyptian and became a fugitive. But look what God did: He not only forgave Moses but the very place where He sent him was the place where he was wanted. God reversed it all. Zero charges were filed when Moses went back to Egypt where he was wanted.

He also used the apostle Paul whose BC (Before Christ) profession was to capture Christians and take them back to Rome to be killed for their allegiance to the Christian faith. He also, the scripture says, consented to the death of Stephen (Acts 22:20). Paul was confessing.

Yet God used him mightily in the spreading of the NT church and the NT scriptures. God even changed his name from Saul to Paul. After coming to Christ, he was a new person and was of a new representation.

The psalmist said in the book of Psalms one hundred and three and verse twelve *"As far as the east is from the west, so far hath he removed our transgressions from us."*

The Psalmist, David was a murderer when he ordered the death of Uriah, his innocent and faithful soldier. Examine second Samuel eleven, verse fifteen: *And he wrote in the letter, saying, **Set ye Uriah in the forefront of the hottest battle**, and retire ye from him, that he may be smitten, and die.*

There is no room for coincidence in this detail. **Murder, conspiracy to commit murder, premeditated hire for murder, presidential abuse of power** was in this detail. However, examine Psalm 51 and observe the true repentance and confession to God by the murder, David.

Also remember that this is the same man whom God, Himself said of David is **the man after His own heart**. Examine God's commentary on David in the book of Acts thirteen verse twenty two: *And when he had removed him, he raised up unto them David to be their king; to **whom also he gave testimony, and said, I have found David the son of Jesse, a man after mine own heart**, which shall fulfill all my will.*

Other Source:
What God says about abortion, Focus On The Family.
The pain that follows, Life Cycle Books
Four Quick Questions, Life Cycle Books
The Holy Bible, King James Version

Index

were fashioned 17
What is over is the baby's life 10
who maketh the dumb, or deaf 24
Why hast thou made me thus? 25
woman forget her sucking 28
work of the law written in their hearts 12

Y

ye that labour and are heavy laden 29

www.ingramcontent.com/pod-product-compliance
Lightning Source LLC
Chambersburg PA
CBHW060643030426
42337CB00018B/3425